Illustrator:
Kathy Bruce

Editor:
Evan D. Forbes, M.S. Ed.

Editor-in-Chief:
Sharon Coan, M.S. Ed.

Art Director:
Elayne Roberts

Cover Artist:
Keith Vasconcelles

Imaging:
David Bennett

Product Manager:
Phil Garcia

Publishers:
Rachelle Cracchiolo, M.S. Ed.
Mary Dupuy Smith, M.S. Ed.

WORLD GEOGRAPHY SERIES
AFRICA

BASED ON NEW NATIONAL GEOGRAPHY STANDARDS
(This series can be purchased as a complete volume or as seven separate continent books.)

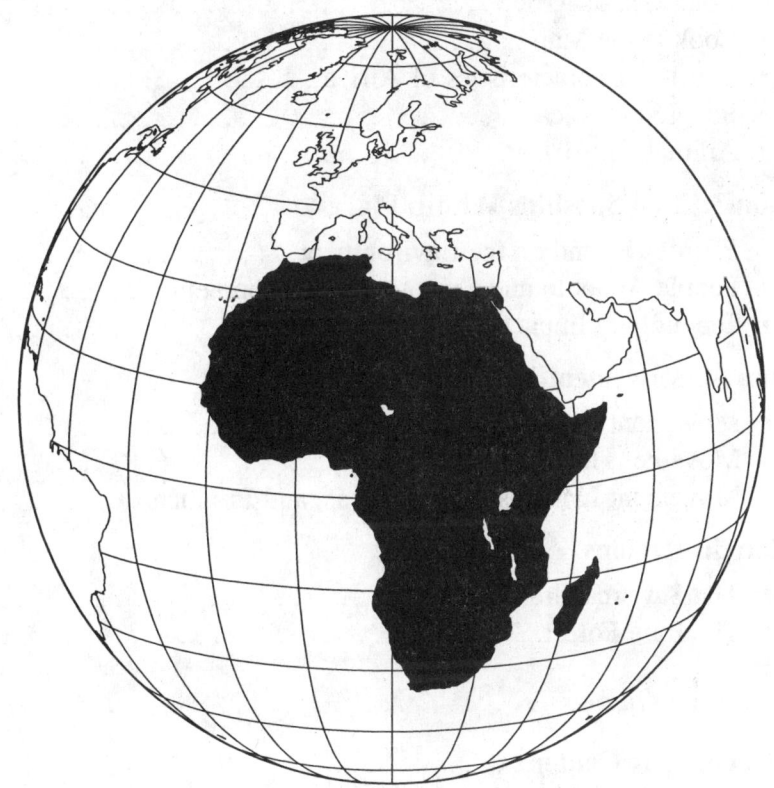

Author:

Julia Jasmine, M.A.

Teacher Created Materials, Inc.
P.O. Box 1040
Huntington Beach, CA 92647
ISBN-1-55734-695-1

©1995 Teacher Created Materials, Inc.   Made in U.S.A.

The classroom teacher may reproduce copies of materials in this book for classroom use only. The reproduction of any part for an entire school or school system is strictly prohibited. No part of this publication may be transmitted, stored, or recorded in any form without written permission from the publisher.

Table of Contents

Introduction 3

Section 1: Location
- A Word or Two About Maps 6
- Where on Earth Is Africa? 9
- Where in Africa Is_____? 14

Section 2: Place
- Countries of Africa 15
- Look at the Map 21
- Physical Characteristics of Africa 22
- People in Africa 26
- Animals in Africa 28

Section 3: Relationships Within Places
- People Depend on the Environment 29
- People Adapt to and Change the Environment 31
- Technology Impacts the Environment 33

Section 4: Movement
- Movement Demonstrates Interdependence 35
- Movement Involves Linkages 37
- Movement Includes People, Ideas, and Products 39

Section 5: Regions
- The Savanna Grasslands 41
- The Rain Forest 45

African Fact Game 47

The Geography Center 52

The Culminating Activity: Making a Book 56

Glossary 71

Software Review 77

Bibliography 78

Answer Key 80

#695 Africa   2   *©1995 Teacher Created Materials, Inc.*

Introduction

What Has Happened to Geography?

Studies made during the last couple of decades show geography as a neglected science, even physical geography, its most traditional form. One of the suspected causes has been the higher priority of teaching subjects like math and science in the classroom. There have been many well-publicized surveys showing that people in the United States are not very well informed about the Earth they live on. Large numbers of people—including students on campuses of important universities where some of the best-publicized surveys have been conducted—were unable to identify the three largest countries on the North American continent, find Florida on a United States map, or name the oceans that border the United States on a world map. (Elementary school students love to hear about these surveys because if they are studying geography, they will be able to answer all of the questions that these college students cannot.)

During the years that the study of geography was being set aside in many of our schools in favor of other priorities, the whole focus of geography changed. Geography was once divided into two major categories: physical geography and human geography. Physical geography is concerned with the natural features of the Earth (land, water, and climate), how they relate to each other, and the living organisms, including people, on the Earth. Physical geography is divided into several categories: biogeography, climatology, geomorphology, oceanography, and soil geography. Human geography studies the patterns of human activity and how it relates to the environment around them. Human geography is divided into several categories: cultural, economic, historical, political, population, social, and urban.

It was easy to compare and contrast geography with other sciences such as astronomy, which describes the Earth in relation to its position in space, and geology, which studies the Earth's structure and composition.

Today, however, geography is crossing into other sciences, as well. We are seeing it in cultural anthropology, demographics, ecology, economics, meteorology, sociology, and zoology. Although these remain separate sciences, the lines separating them are more blurry than ever before, and many new approaches to the study of geography are being advocated.

GENIP—A National Project

In 1984, the Association of American Geographers (AAG) together with the National Council for Geographic Education (NCGE) published *Guidelines for Geographic Education: Elementary and Secondary Schools* in which they identified five fundamental themes of geography. These five themes were specifically designed and written to be used by teachers. (Crossland, 1994) In 1987, these two groups were joined by the American Geographical Society (AGS) and the National Geographic Society (NGS) to form the Geographic Education National Implementation Project (GENIP) for the purpose of implementing the aforementioned guidelines and improving the status and quality of geographic education in the United States.

Introduction (cont.)

What Has Happened to Geography? (cont.)

The Five Themes

The first theme is called *Location: Position on the Earth's Surface*. There are two kinds of location: absolute and relative. The absolute, or exact, location of any place on Earth can be specified by giving its latitude and longitude. The relative location of a place is given by describing its relationship to other places. Absolute location is like a street address. ("I live at 2100 Oak Lane, Smalltown, CA 98765.") Relative location is a more qualitative set of directions. ("I live in the white two-story house on the corner across from the tennis courts in the park.")

The second theme is *Place: Physical and Human Characteristics*. These are the characteristics that differentiate one place from another. They include physical characteristics like landforms, bodies of water, climate, and plant and animal life, as well as land use, architecture, language, religion, type of government, and even communication and transportation if they are unique.

The third theme is *Relationships Within Places: Humans and Their Environment*. Here we ask students to take a look at the ways in which people react with their environments. This is important in this age of ecological awareness when we are trying to make good choices about the Earth.

The fourth theme is *Movement: Humans Interacting on the Earth*. This theme focuses on human interdependence. This is where a more general and comprehensive look is taken at transportation and communication.

The fifth and last theme is entitled *Regions: How They Form and Change*. GENIP defines a region as an area with one or more common characteristics or features which give it a measure of unity and make it different from the surrounding areas. The geography of the United States is often divided into a consideration of its regions—Northeast, Southeast, Midwest, Southwest, Rocky Mountain, and Pacific.

A New Mix

These themes are really a new mix of the old physical/human divisions. The first and fifth themes are more "physical" and the second and fourth more "human," while the third theme contains much of the material connected with our concern for the safety of the environment. The chief benefit of this approach may be the freshness it brings to one of the oldest of the academic disciplines. The themes themselves can be taught and discussed in any order or combination.

Introduction (cont.)

Africa

This book was designed to present an overview of the geography of the continent of Africa. It is divided into five sections to match the themes of the Geographic Education National Implementation Project (GENIP), an educational project backed by the nation's most prestigious geographers.

Each section contains a selection of teaching pages, maps, activities, interesting facts, review questions, and puzzles or games. A plan for using the material to construct a geography center is also included, as well as ideas for putting together a book as a culminating activity.

You will also find a glossary of the specialized vocabulary used by geographers. This will make it easier for your students to talk about the world they live in.

Location

A Word or Two About Maps

Projections

The landforms shown on maps and globes do not look exactly alike. This is because it is just as hard to "peel" a globe and flatten the Earth's "skin" out into a map as it is to peel an orange and flatten out its skin to make a smooth, even surface. Even if you can get the skin off the orange in one piece, the top and bottom edges must be broken and spread out.

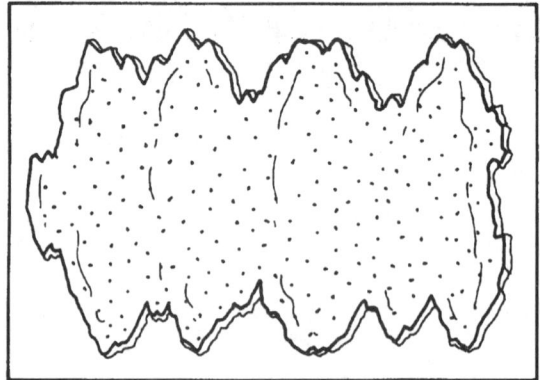

Different map makers (cartographers) have had different ideas about how to do this and have made different "projections." A projection is the way in which the map maker has chosen to flatten out the Earth's surface to make a flat map. Sometimes the map maker allows the breaks in the Earth's surface to show.

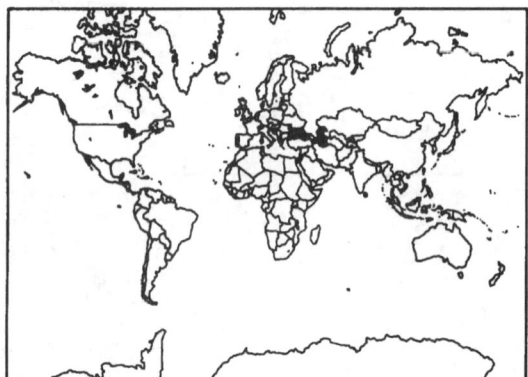

Sometimes the map maker stretches the Earth's "skin." This makes the countries near the poles look much bigger than they really are.

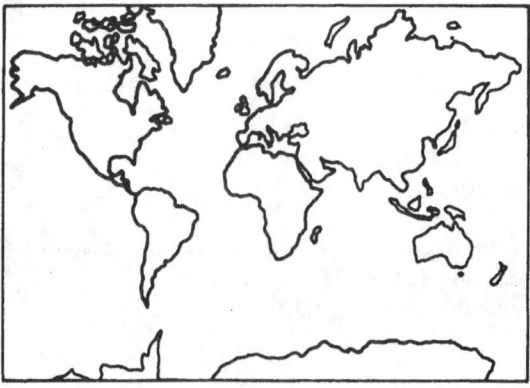

#695 Africa   ©1995 Teacher Created Materials, Inc.

Location

A Word or Two About Maps *(cont.)*

Projections *(cont.)*

Use your reference materials to find out the names of other common map projections and list them below. Research the advantages and disadvantages of each map projection you list and write them down below.

Map Projection	Advantages	Disadvantages

Location

A Word or Two About Maps (cont.)

The Compass Rose

The compass rose is a small drawing that shows direction on a map. Most maps show north at the top and south at the bottom, west on the left and east on the right.

Look at maps to find some different styles of compass roses and then design your own. You can shrink your drawing and make multiple copies to use on the maps you make, color, or label.

#695 Africa   8   ©1995 Teacher Created Materials, Inc.

Location

Where on Earth Is Africa?

- Africa lies between the Atlantic Ocean and the Indian Ocean.
- Africa is the second largest continent, smaller only than Asia.
- The equator runs through the center of Africa.
- The Mediterranean Sea and the Red Sea form the northern boundaries of Africa.

Use these clues to find Africa on this map. Color it blue.

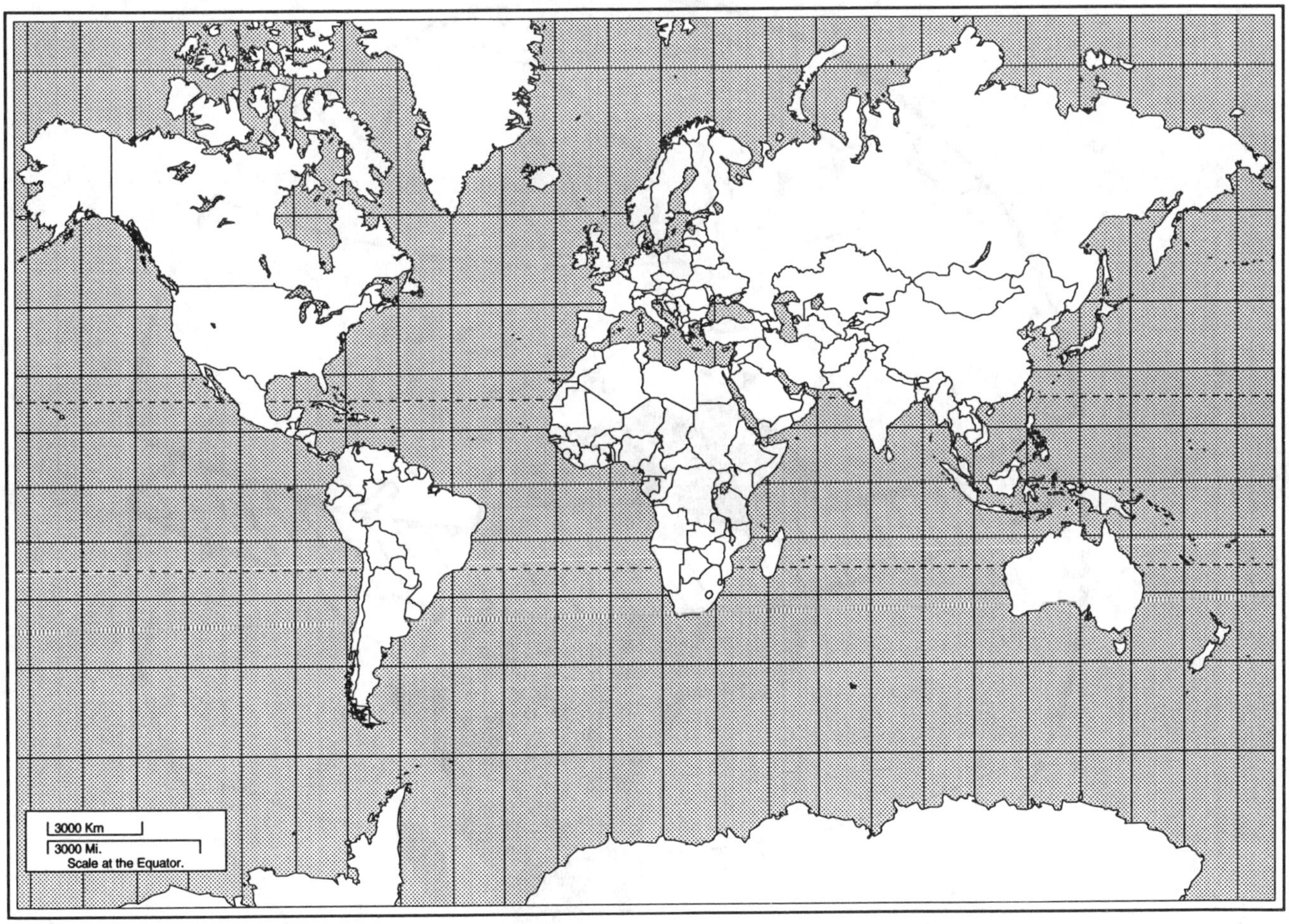

©1995 Teacher Created Materials, Inc.   9   #695 Africa

Location

Where on Earth Is Africa? (cont.)

If you think of the Earth as a ball (a sphere or globe), you can draw a line around the middle (the equator) and separate the two halves into the top half (Northern Hemisphere) and the bottom half (Southern Hemisphere). Now you can talk about something as being in the Northern or Southern Hemisphere.

More lines are drawn around the Earth parallel to the equator and evenly spaced from the equator to the North and South Poles. They are called parallels or lines of latitude. They are numbered in degrees, starting with 0° at the equator and usually spaced at 15° intervals, ending with 90° N at the North Pole and 90° S at the South Pole.

(Geographers further divide their degrees into minutes and seconds so they can be very precise in locating the position of anything on the Earth's surface.)

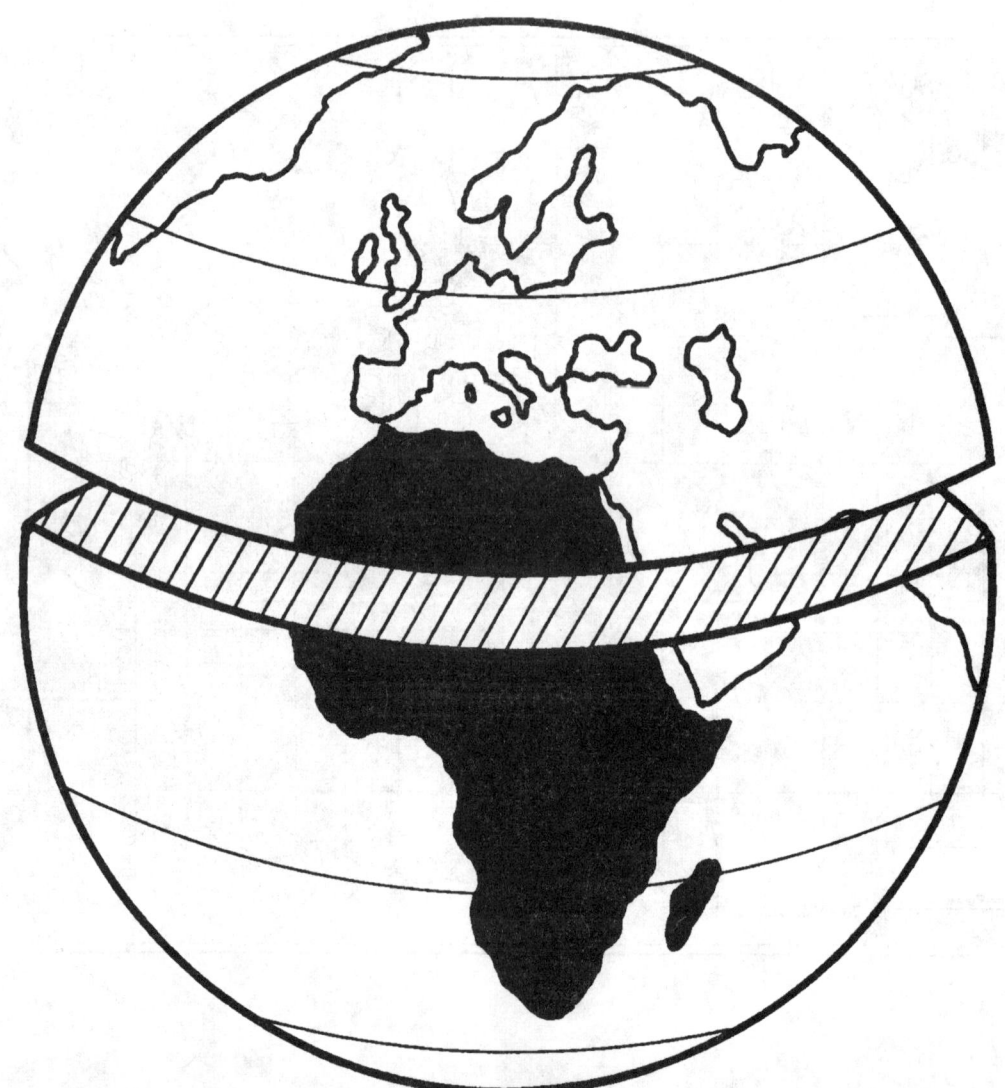

If you divide the Earth into its Northern and Southern Hemispheres, Africa lies in the _____ Hemisphere and in the _____ Hemisphere.

Location

Where on Earth Is Africa? *(cont.)*

You can also draw lines north and south around the Earth. These lines are called meridians or lines of longitude. They are usually shown 15° apart at the equator, but they all come together at the North and South Poles. (They also can be further divided into minutes and seconds, just like the parallels.)

The line that runs through Greenwich, England, is called the prime meridian (0°). Longitude is the distance east or west of the prime meridian. The line directly opposite the prime meridian is at 180° and is called the date line. If you are still thinking of the Earth as a ball (a sphere or globe), you can separate the two halves into the Western Hemisphere and the Eastern Hemisphere. (This is usually done along the meridians of 20° W and 160° E so all of Africa is in one hemisphere.)

If you divide the Earth into its Western and Eastern Hemisphere, Africa is in the _____ Hemisphere.

©1995 Teacher Created Materials, Inc.   11   #695 Africa

Location

Where on Earth Is Africa? *(cont.)*

You can tell where things on the Earth are in two ways:

- You can give their exact or absolute location using latitude and longitude expressed in degrees (minutes and seconds).
- You can tell where they are in relation to other things.

Fill out the missing information to give the exact location of where you live:

house number	street name	apartment number
city	state/country	zip code

Now, use information from a map or globe to complete this description of the exact location of Africa.

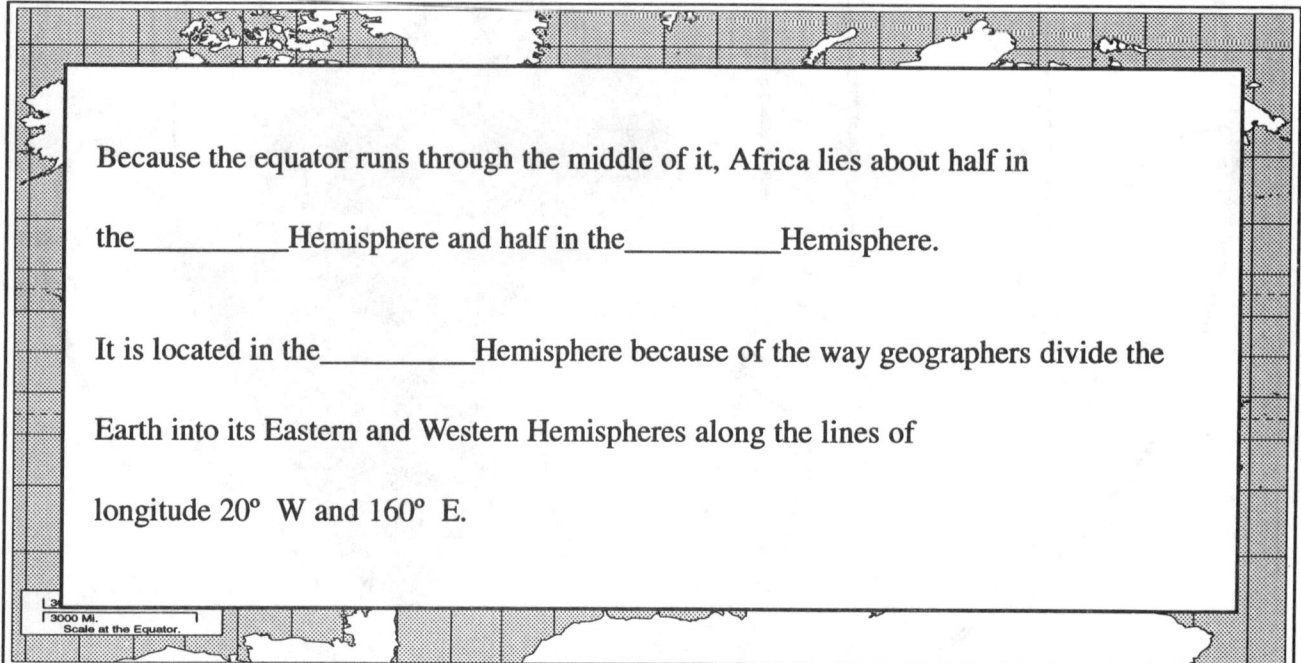

Because the equator runs through the middle of it, Africa lies about half in the _____ Hemisphere and half in the _____ Hemisphere.

It is located in the _____ Hemisphere because of the way geographers divide the Earth into its Eastern and Western Hemispheres along the lines of longitude 20° W and 160° E.

Location

Where on Earth Is Africa? *(cont.)*

You can tell where things on the Earth are in two ways:

- You can give their exact or absolute location using latitude and longitude expressed in degrees (minutes and seconds).
- You can tell where they are in relation to other things.

Fill out the missing information of where you live in relation to other things:

I live

between_____and_____

near_____

and across

from_____.

Now, use the information from a map or globe to complete this description of the relative location of Africa.

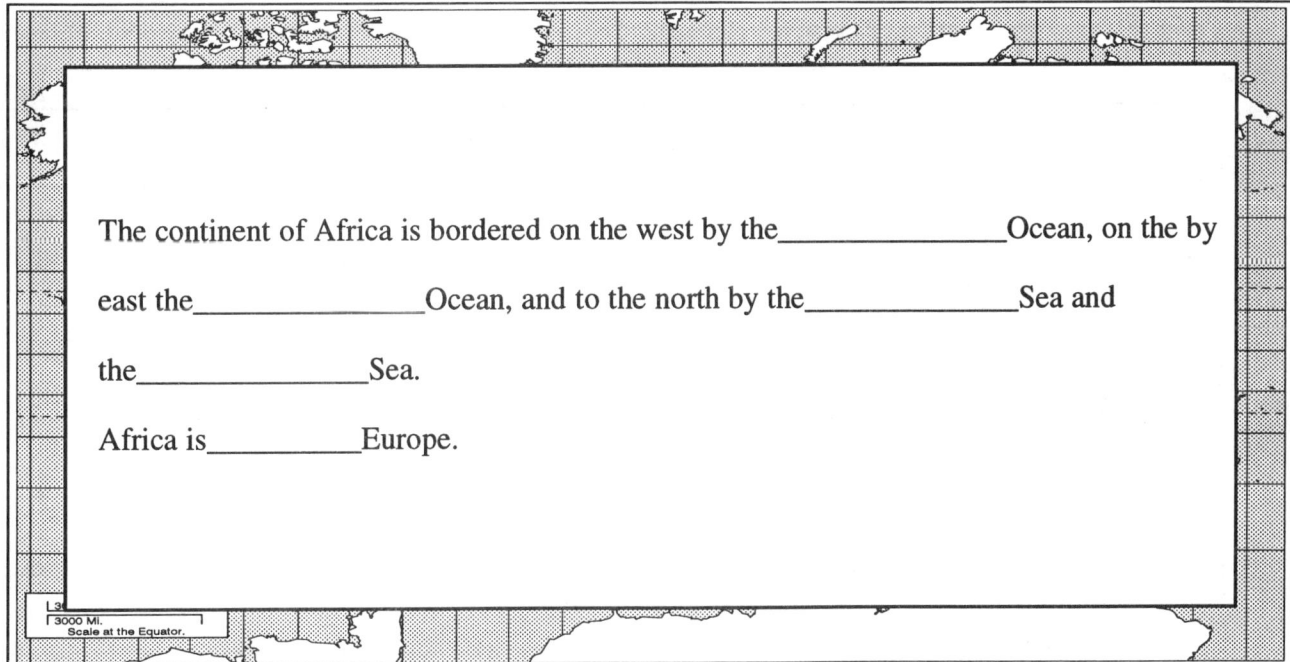

The continent of Africa is bordered on the west by the_____Ocean, on the by east the_____Ocean, and to the north by the_____Sea and the_____Sea.

Africa is_____Europe.

©1995 Teacher Created Materials, Inc.

Location

Where in Africa Is ____?

Use information from a globe or map, an atlas, an encyclopedia, and your geography book to write both the exact and relative locations of five of the countries on the African continent. See the next page for the names of countries to choose from.

1. _____
   _____
   _____
   _____

2. _____
   _____
   _____
   _____

3. _____
   _____
   _____
   _____

4. _____
   _____
   _____
   _____

5. _____
   _____
   _____
   _____

Place

Countries of Africa

There are 51 countries of Africa listed below. Find them forwards, backwards, and diagonally in the word search below.

```
L M O R O C C O T H E G A M B I A G U I N E A S
I O A N G O L A L G E R I A A N E L E H T S S O
B Z Q W T E R T M G U I N E A B I S S A U O I U
Y A Y S A O T O M E A N D P R I N C I P E M E T
A M U I O E G Y P T R P L K E R I T R E A A R H
A B E N I N Z O X C V O S E N E G A L B Z L R A
Z I M B A B W E E T H I O P I A E N M M A I A F
Q Q W E R T Y U M I N O I N U E R A S D M A L R
F U G H E Q U A T O R I A L G U I N E A B J E I
C E N T R A L A F R I C A N R E P U B L I C O C
I M A U R I T A N I A M H S N B V U C X A O N A
V Q W N I G E R I A R R O A N T R Y U P I N E S
O E L I B E R I A S D R F O D K G H E J K G M W
R M N S U D A N V C O X B Z I A E V S D F O A A
Y D J I B O U T I M U A Q N W E E N R T Y H U Z
C A Z A I R E S O D G H A N A R F G Y D F T R I
O M N B V Z X C Z A A F S D D I W A L A M O I L
A Q T A N Z A N I A N E R E T Y U A K J H S T A
S M A Y O B T E A S D S D F B U R U N D I E I N
T N A M I B I A O G A B O T S W A N A D H L U D
S E Y C H E L L E S A E M A D A G A S C A R S D
```

Cross off the countries as you find them: Morocco, Algeria, Tunisia, Mauritania, Mali, Niger, Libya, Egypt, Chad, Sudan, Cape Verde, Senegal, Gambia, Guinea-Bissau, Guinea, Sierra Leone, Liberia, Ghana, Togo, Benin, Nigeria, Cameroon, Central African Republic, Sao Tome and Principe, Equatorial Guinea, Gabon, Congo, Zaire, Angola, Ethiopia, Djibouti, Somalia, Uganda, Kenya, Rwanda, Burundi, Tanzania, Seychelles, Comoros, Madagascar, Mauritius, Zambia, Malawi, Mozambique, Namibia, Botswana, Zimbabwe, South Africa, Swaziland, Lesotho, Eritrea

Place

Countries of Africa (cont.)

Use information from an atlas, an encyclopedia, your geography book, or any other reference book to write two interesting facts about each African country listed below.

1. Algeria _____
   _____

2. Angola _____
   _____

3. Benin _____
   _____

4. Botswana _____
   _____

5. Burkina Faso _____
   _____

6. Burundi _____
   _____

7. Cameroon _____
   _____

8. Cape Verde _____
   _____

9. Central African Republic _____
   _____

10. Chad _____
    _____

11. Comoros _____
    _____

#695 Africa   ©1995 Teacher Created Materials, Inc.

Place

Countries of Africa (cont.)

12. Congo _____
_____

13. Ivory Coast _____
_____

14. Djibouti _____
_____

15. Egypt _____
_____

16. Equatorial Guinea _____
_____

17. Ethiopia _____
_____

18. Gabon _____
_____

19. Ghana _____
_____

20. Guinea _____
_____

21. Guinea-Bissau _____
_____

22. Kenya _____
_____

©1995 Teacher Created Materials, Inc.　　　　17　　　　#695 Africa

Place

Countries of Africa *(cont.)*

23. Lesotho _____
_____

24. Liberia _____
_____

25. Libya _____
_____

26. Madagascar _____
_____

27. Malawi _____
_____

28. Mali _____
_____

29. Mauritania _____
_____

30. Mauritius _____
_____

31. Morocco _____
_____

32. Mozambique _____
_____

33. Namibia _____
_____

34. Niger _____
_____

Countries of Africa (cont.)

35. Nigeria _____

_____

36. Rwanda _____

_____

37. São Tome and Principe _____

_____

38. Senegal _____

_____

39. Seychelles _____

_____

40. Sierra Leone _____

_____

41. Somalia _____

_____

42. South Africa _____

_____

43. Sudan _____

_____

44. Swaziland _____

_____

45. Tanzania _____

_____

Place

Countries of Africa *(cont.)*

46. Gambia _____

_____

47. Togo _____

_____

48. Tunisia _____

_____

49. Uganda _____

_____

50. Zaire _____

_____

51. Zambia _____

_____

52. Zimbabwe _____

_____

Bonus!

Many African nations changed their names when they became countries that colonized. How many can you find? What were their old names? What are they called now?

_____
_____
_____
_____
_____
_____

Place

Look at the Map

Use the numbered list of African countries on pages 16-20 to label the map below. Write the number of each country on the map and use the list for a key.

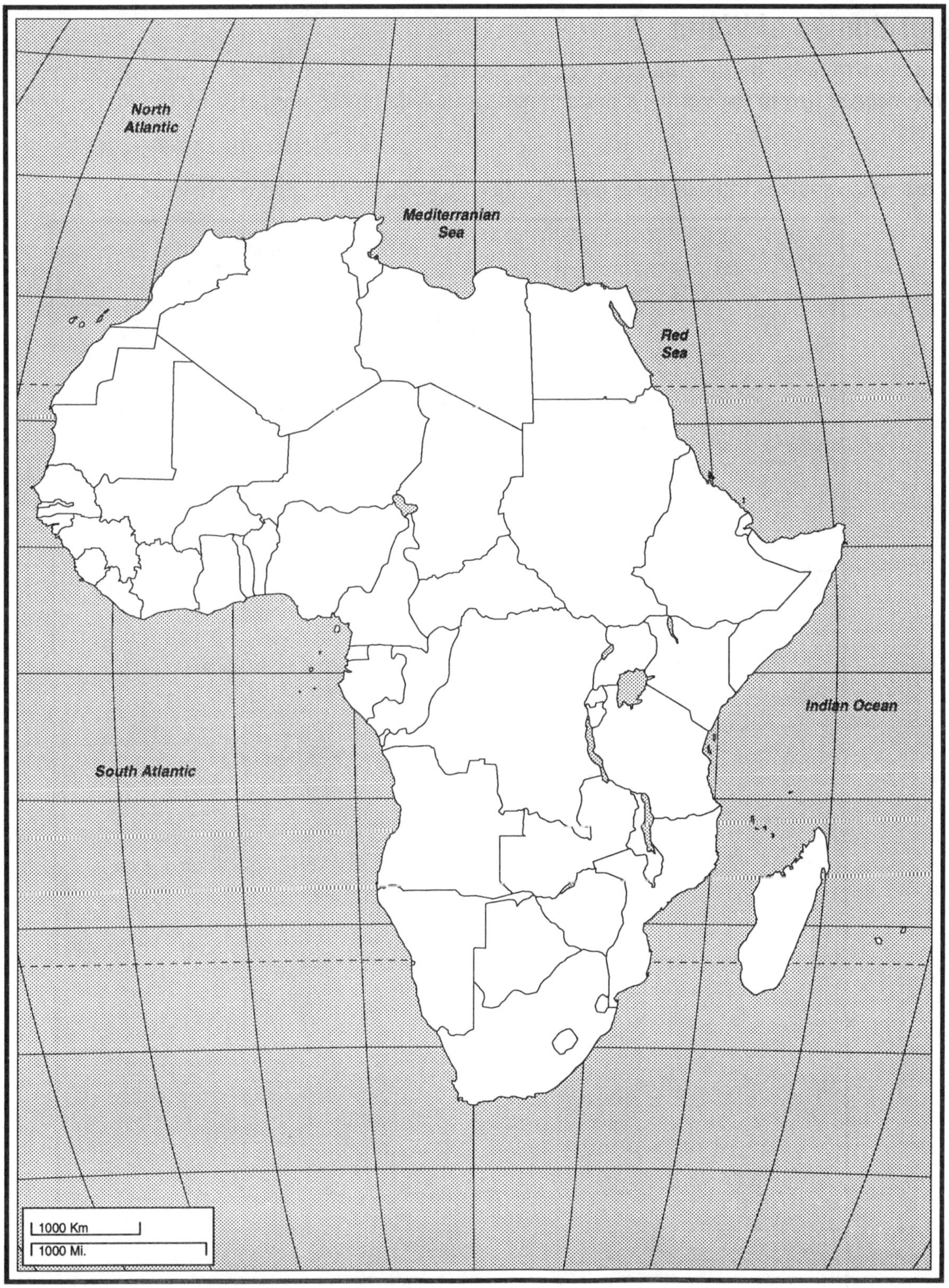

©1995 Teacher Created Materials, Inc.   #695 Africa

Place

Physical Characteristics of Africa

Major Bodies of Water

Africa is surrounded by the *Atlantic Ocean* to the west, the *Indian Ocean* to the east, and the *Mediterranean Sea* to the north. It is separated from Asia on the northeast by the *Red Sea* and the *Gulf of Aden*.

Use reference sources to label these major bodies of water on the map of Africa.

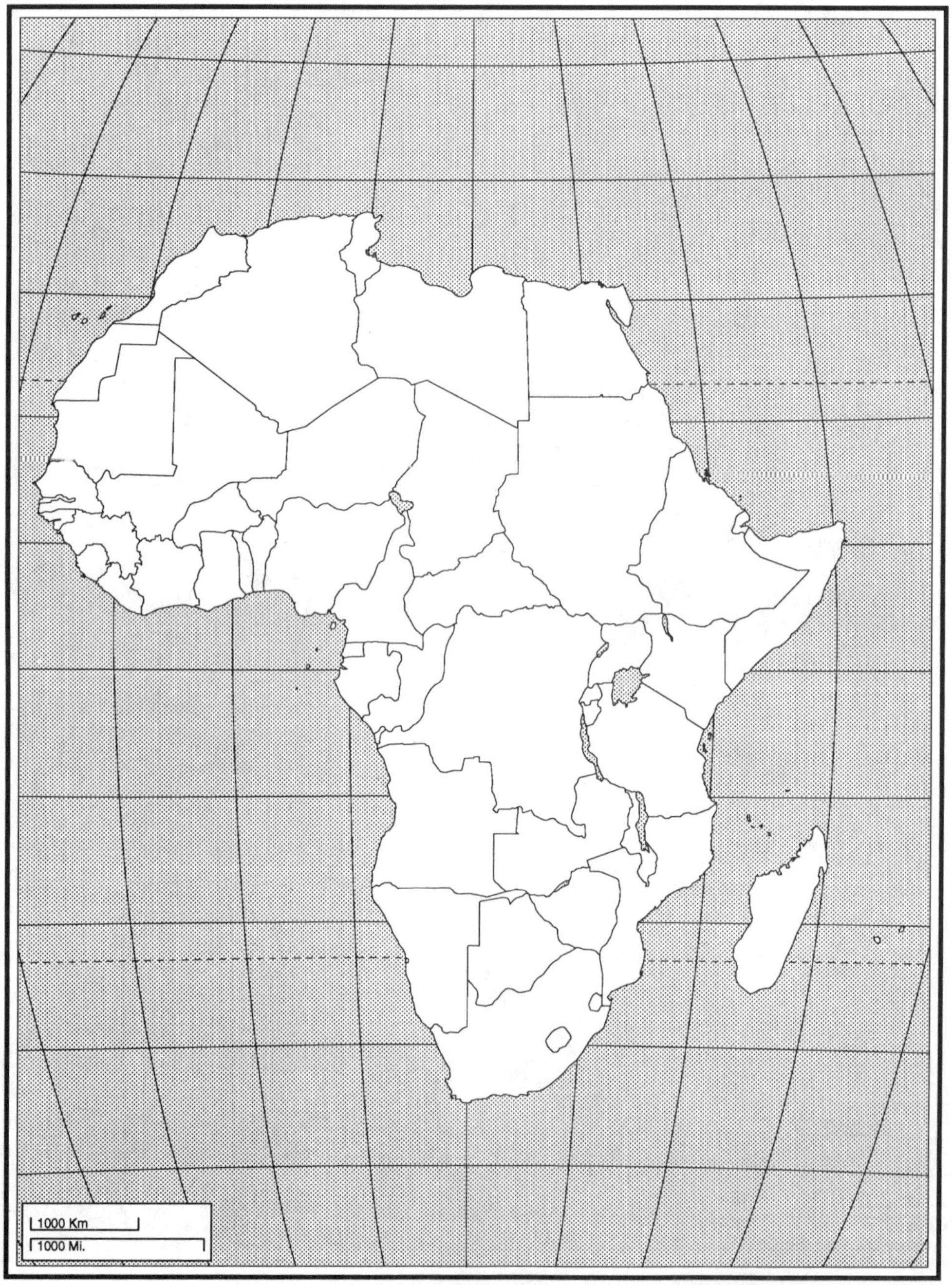

Place

Physical Characteristics of Africa (cont.)

Landforms

Africa is the second largest continent. Its coastlines are not as irregular as those of the other continents, and it has fewer mountains. *The Atlas Mountains* border on the Mediterranean Sea. *Mount Kilimanjaro,* the highest point in Africa, is a volcanic peak that rises near the east coast of the continent. Mount Kilimanjaro is near the *Great Rift Valley,* which runs north and south from the *Ethiopian Highlands* near the Red Sea almost to the Malawi River. This is an area where two of the Earth's plates are pulling apart, making a long wide depression on the Earth's surface.

Africa is largely desert. The *Sahara* sweeps across the north of Africa, filling more than a quarter of the continent. The *Sahel*, which is an arid grassland bordering the Sahara on the south, is turning into desert too. The *Kalahari Desert* and the *Namib Desert* cover much of southern Africa. In the middle of the continent, centered on the Equator, lies the *Congo Basin* covered with a rain forest that is one of the wettest places on Earth. Between the rain forest and the deserts are the savanna grasslands and great plains, which are home to most of Africa's large animals. The island of Madagascar is also part of Africa. It lies about 150 miles (240 km) off the southeast coast and is considered a continental fragment.

Use reference sources to label these landforms on the map of Africa.

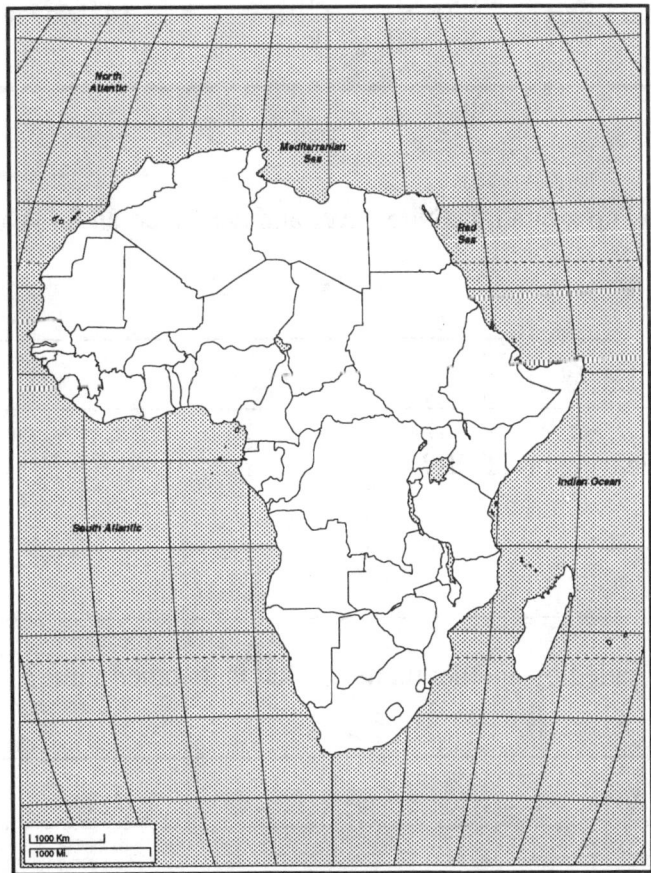

Place

Physical Characteristics of Africa *(cont.)*

Other Bodies of Water

Africa has important lakes and rivers. The *Nile* is the longest river in the world, with a length of 4,145 miles (6,632 km). Other important rivers are the *Niger*, the *Congo*, the *Zambezi*, the *Senegal*, and the *Orange*. Lakes include *Victoria* and *Tanganyika*, two of the largest in the world. The *Mozambique Channel* divides Madagascar from the mainland.

Using reference sources and the map on page 25, draw the lakes and rivers listed below. Then label those lakes, rivers, and bodies of water with their numbers and use the list for a key.

---

1. Lake Tanganyika
2. Lake Victoria
3. Lake Malawi
4. Lake Chad
5. Lake Volta
6. Congo River
7. Zambezi River
8. Senegal River
9. Orange River
10. Niger River
11. Nile River
12. White Nile River
13. Blue Nile River
14. Mozambique Channel

Bonus Questions!

What ancient country grew up around the Nile River and depended on its yearly flooding for planting crops?

_____

_____

On which river will you find Victoria Falls?

_____

_____

Which river is sometimes called by another name? What is its other name?

_____

_____

#695 Africa   24   ©1995 Teacher Created Materials, Inc.

Place

Physical Characteristics of Africa *(cont.)*

Other Bodies of Water

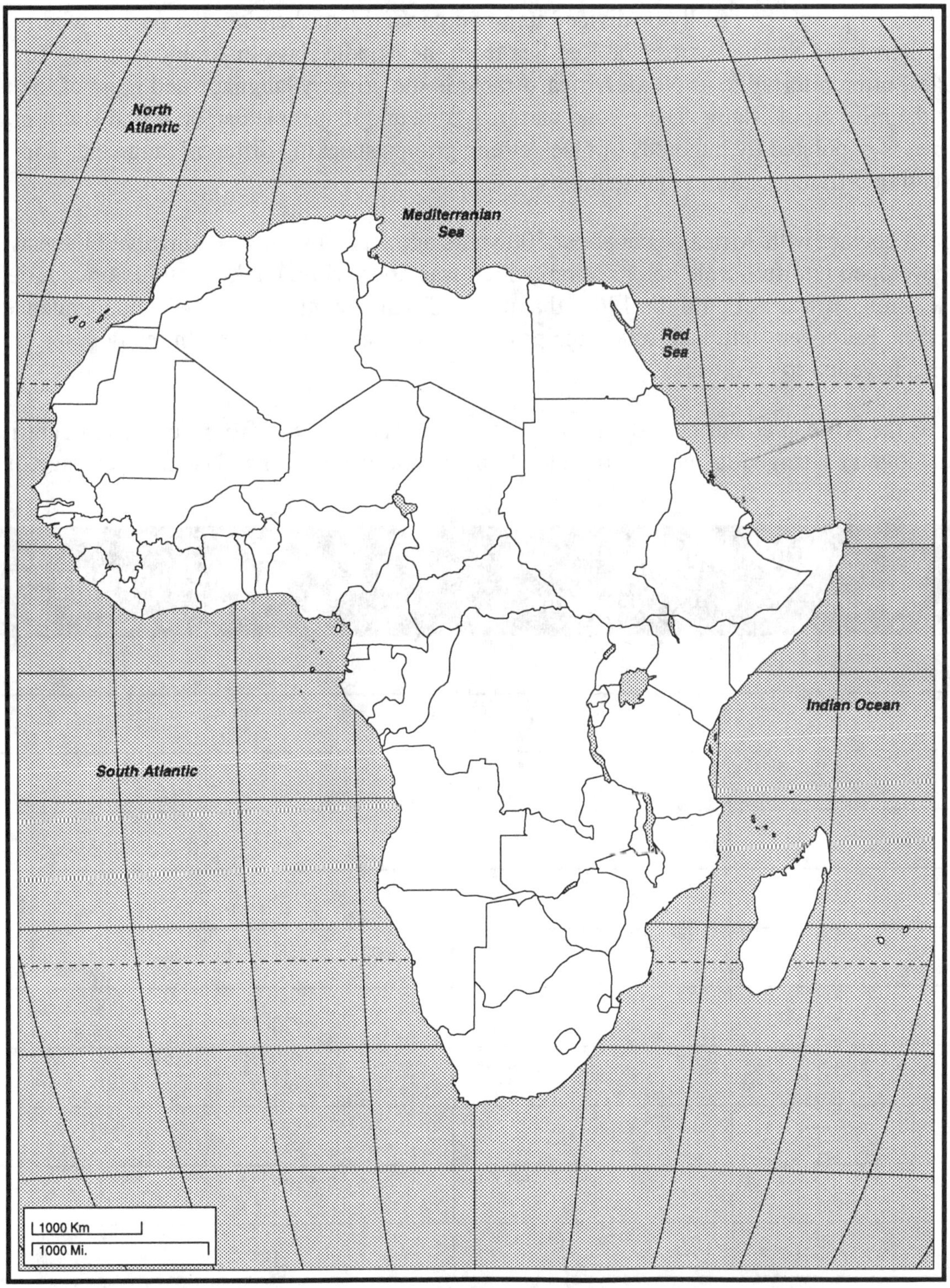

Place

People in Africa

The oldest human fossils have been found in Africa, in Olduvai Gorge, which is located in the Great Rift Valley. Africa may turn out to be the place where the human race began. Certainly, many great civilizations developed there. Egypt is well known, of course. But, when Europeans first came to Africa, Timbuktu, in what is now Mali, was also a center of commerce and learning, as was Zimbabwe in the southeast.

Africa and its people can really be divided into two parts. First, there are the people who live around the Mediterranean Sea and across the Red Sea from the Middle Eastern Arab countries. In these countries, often referred to as North Africa, Arabic is the primary language and most of the people follow the religion of Islam. The second part of Africa and its people can be found south of the Sahara. This area is populated by hundreds of black ethnic groups speaking different languages and representing different cultures and religions.

European contact with Africa began about 500 years ago. The first contact involved the slave trade but soon developed into full-scale colonization, which was done without taking ethnic boundaries into consideration. It was not until the 1960s that most African countries won their independence and, when most of the Europeans left, had to face the problems of ethnic boundaries. In many cases, these problems have led to civil wars.

Research the African countries that have declared their independence from European countries. If the African country changed its name, write the old name and the new one. Use another page, if you need more room.

African Country		European Country
Old Name	New Name	

Place

People in Africa (cont.)

Ethnic Groups

Pick an African ethnic group to learn about and answer these questions. Some suggested groups are listed below.

Arabs   **Pygmies**   **Masai**   **Ibo**

1. In which African environment does this group of people live?

2. Do they live the way their ancestors lived? If not, what changes have they made?

3. What are their homes like?

4. How do they earn a living? (What kind of work do they do?)

5. What religion do they practice?

6. Use the back of this page to tell about some of their customs.

Place

Animals in Africa

Read the clues and unscramble the names of African animals. Circle the names of the animals that are on the endangered species list.

1. _____ large and ferocious-looking but really shy and friendly animals who live in both the lowlands and mountains (larislog)

2. _____ an animal easily recognized by its long neck (feragif)

3. _____ the pack animal of North Africa (macel)

4. _____ a large animal with a long trunk and two curving tusks (pantheel)

5. _____ a fierce carnivore of the grasslands (nilo)

6. _____ a spotted cat of the forests and plains (paroled)

7. _____ a type of anteater (radavkra)

8. _____ its name means river horse (pathopmipuso)

9. _____ an animal that is almost extinct because it is hunted for its horns (conshorier)

10. _____ a monkey that may have colorful markings on its body (bobnoa)

11. _____ is it black with white stripes or white with black stripes (razeb)

12. _____ there are many varieties of this grass-eating animal (lopteena)

13. _____ an animal that looks a lot like a raccoon (trielading muerl)

14. _____ an animal that is often confused with the alligator (dilorcoce)

15. _____ the ape that is ranked as the most intelligent of all animals (pamnizeech)

#695 Africa   28   ©1995 Teacher Created Materials, Inc.

Relationships

People Depend on the Environment

Make a list of Africa's natural resources.

_____
_____
_____
_____
_____

Then, create a symbol to go with each natural resource and make a key. Using your newly created symbols, show these resources on the map of Africa on the next page.

Resource Key

Relationships

People Depend on the Environment *(cont.)*

Resource Map

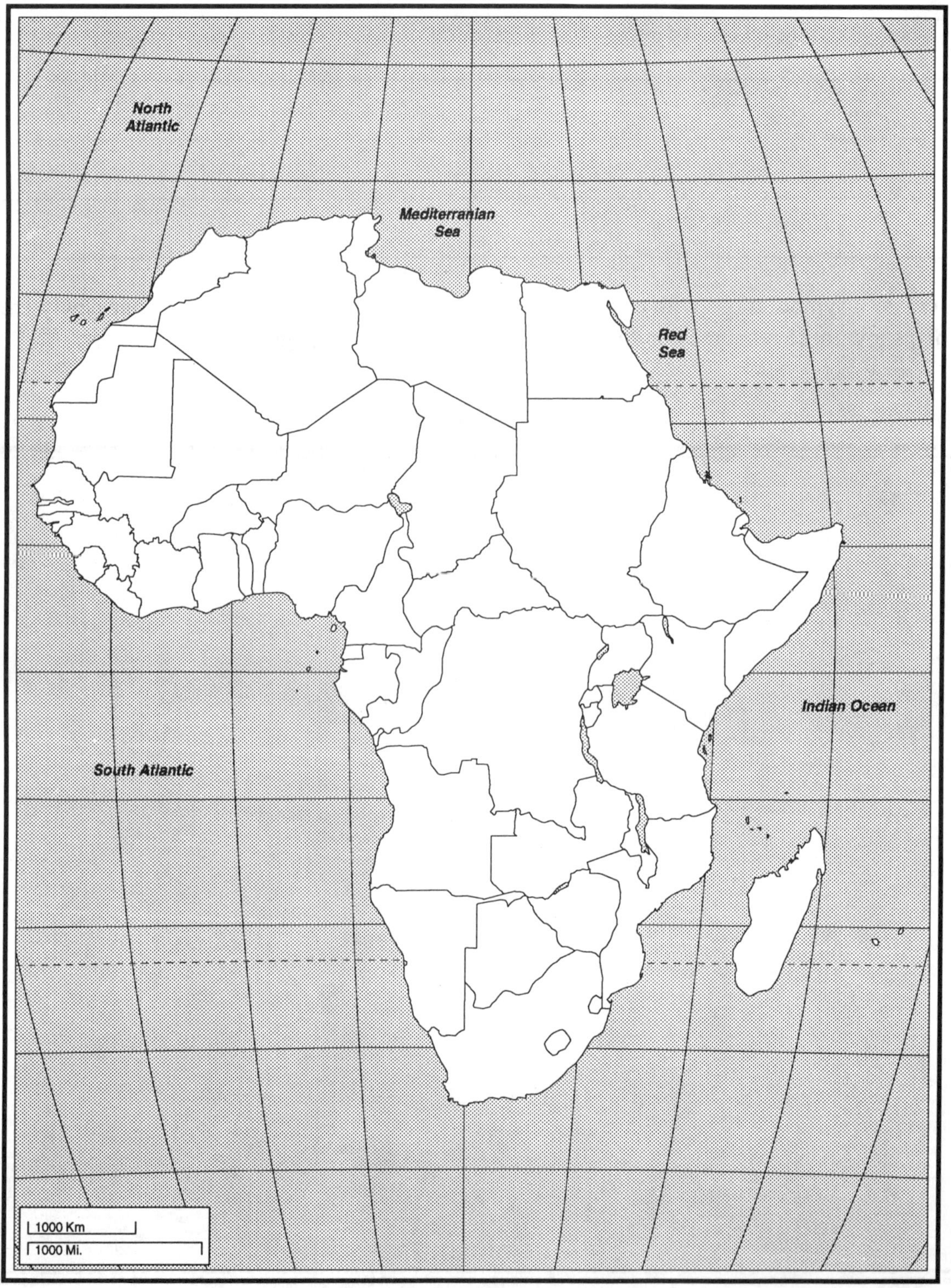

Relationships

People Adapt to and Change the Environment

People adapt to and change the environment in many ways. Think of some possible solutions that may solve these environmental problems:

Very dry conditions for farming:

_____
_____
_____
_____

Hills too steep for crops:

_____
_____
_____
_____

Areas that flood:

_____
_____
_____
_____

Housing in hot climates:

_____
_____
_____
_____

People Adapt to and Change the Environment *(cont.)*

People adapt to and change the environment in many ways. Think of some possible solutions that may solve these environmental problems:

Housing in cold climates:

_____
_____
_____
_____

Clothing in hot climates:

_____
_____
_____
_____

Clothing in cold climates:

_____
_____
_____
_____

Transportation in mountainous or hilly areas:

_____
_____
_____
_____

Relationships

Technology Impacts the Environment

Resources are things that are valued and used by people. Natural resources are resources that occur in nature, such as minerals in the Earth, trees, water, and air.

The way people feel about and use natural resources changes as new technologies are developed. However, the development and application of these technologies is affected by several factors: wealth, organization, and infrastructure. Infrastructure is what underlies new development. It consists of things like sewers, power sources and power lines, water purification plants, roads, tunnels, and bridges.

Work with a partner or in a group to figure out what kinds of infrastructure are needed for the uses of technology listed below.

Technology	Infrastructure Needed
Bathrooms with running water and flush toilets	
Radio reception	
Television reception	

©1995 Teacher Created Materials, Inc.   33   #695 Africa

Technology Impacts the Environment (cont.)

Work with a partner or in a group to figure out what kinds of infrastructure are needed for the uses of technology listed below.

Technology	Infrastructure Needed
Telephones	
Lights	
Train transportation	
Car and truck transportation	
Machines to assist with farming	

Movement

Movement Demonstrates Interdependence

Why does human activity require movement? _____
_____
_____

Do the people in your family go places? _____ Choose two people and answer the following questions:

	Person #1	Person #2
Who?		
When?		
Where?		
How far?		
How often?		
Why?		
Mode of transportation?		

Movement Demonstrates Interdependence (cont.)

Use reference sources to figure the distances between these African cities.

Algiers/Tunis _____

Cairo/Khartoum _____

Cape Town/Tripoli _____

Nairobi/Pretoria _____

Bangui/Mogadisho _____

Brazzaville/Rabat _____

Addis Ababa/Accra _____

Alexandria/Djibouti _____

Casablanca/Tripoli _____

Asmara/Abuja _____

Kampala/Kinshasa _____

Windhoek/Gaborone _____

Addis Ababa 2600 km
Tunis 2750 km
Nairobi 3060 km
Capetown 5130 km

Movement

Movement Involves Linkages

List some of the ways people travel from place to place in the less developed regions of Africa.

_____
_____
_____
_____
_____
_____

List some of the ways people travel from place to place in the urban areas of Africa.

_____
_____
_____
_____
_____
_____

Bonus Question!

Why don't many people use cars to travel from one city to another?

_____
_____
_____
_____
_____
_____
_____

Movement Involves Linkages (cont.)

How will people travel around Africa in the future?

_____
_____
_____
_____

Design your own future method of transportation. Explain it and then draw a picture of it below.

_____
_____
_____
_____

This Is How My Future Transportation Will Work:

_____
_____
_____
_____

This Is How My Future Transportation Will Look:

Movement

Movement Includes People, Ideas, and Products

People go places for business and for pleasure. Going somewhere for pleasure is called touring.

Where have you gone for pleasure?

_____
_____
_____
_____

Where would you like to go?

_____
_____
_____
_____

Ideas can travel too. List some of the different ways ideas travel from place to place.

_____
_____
_____
_____

Products also travel. What are some of the ways products travel?

_____
_____
_____
_____

Movement

Includes People, Ideas, and Products *(cont.)*

Think about a place you would like to visit in Africa. Design a cover for a travel brochure about that place. Sketch your design below. Write a description of the place that will make other people want to travel there too.

_____
_____
_____
_____
_____

Regions

Savanna Grasslands

Animals Across the Curriculum

A region is a portion of the Earth's surface that has characteristics unlike any other. The savannas of Africa form a region. They are flat, sunny plains covered with long, thick grass and dotted with few trees. Most of the large animals of Africa live there.

Africa has more kinds of grassland animals than any other continent. The *elephant*, *rhinoceros*, and *hippopotamus* are three of the largest. The *giraffe* and *zebra* also live on the savannas, along with the *ostrich, aardvark, kudu, gnu,* and many other varieties of *antelope*. The *lion* is probably the best known and most ferocious of all African grassland animals.

1. **The Elephant**

Be ready to report on the elephant. Find out what this animal eats, if it migrates, and if its territory has become smaller. Write down any other facts that you think are interesting.

_____
_____
_____
_____
_____

2. **The Giraffe**

Write a poem about the giraffe. This gentle, awkward-looking animal would seem like something out of a science-fiction story if we were not so used to what they look like. Try to see a video tape or read an illustrated book about this animal before you write your poem. Write your title and poem here and use another piece of paper to illustrate your poem when it is finished.

_____
_____
_____
_____
_____

Regions

The Savanna Grasslands (cont.)

Animals Across the Curriculum

3. Put the names of the italicized animals on page 41 in ABC order and tell how many syllables are in each one.

4. **The Hippopotamus and the Rhinoceros**

   Compare and contrast these two huge animals. Where do they live? What do they eat? How much do they weigh? Do they have any enemies? What other interesting facts can you find out?

   _____
   _____
   _____
   _____
   _____
   _____
   _____
   _____
   _____

Regions

The Savanna Grasslands *(cont.)*

Animals Across the Curriculum *(cont.)*

5. The Aardvark

The aardvark is a kind of anteater. Anteaters live in many places and go by many names. How is the aardvark different from the giant anteater or ant bear, the collared anteater, the echidna, and the pangolin? Find out as much information as you can about anteaters and list it below.

_____

_____

_____

_____

_____

_____

_____

_____

_____

_____

_____

_____

_____

_____

_____

_____

_____

_____

_____

_____

Regions

The Savanna Grasslands *(cont.)*

Animals Across the Curriculum *(cont.)*

6. Antelopes

How many kinds of antelopes live on the African savannas? What do they look like? How can you tell them apart?

_____
_____
_____

7. A Bar Graph

Many African countries are setting aside land for game reserves. Pick six countries and use a bar graph to compare their total land area with the land they have set aside for wild animals. Keep track of your facts here as you do your research.

Country	Total Land Area	Wild Animal Reserves

Regions

The Rain Forest

The Congo Basin lies on the equator in the middle of Africa, right where the continent narrows down on the Atlantic side near the Gulf of Guinea. Here is where the African rain forest grows. This is one of the wettest places on Earth; rain falls almost every day of the year. The rain forest covers a much smaller area than either the African deserts or the grasslands. The Congo River and its tributaries flow through it, and the basin is always hot and humid. The rain forest is still home to many exotic animals, but many of its native animals now live only in zoos around the world.

Find information about this area in reference books and answer these questions.

1. How long is the Congo River?

   _____

2. What is unique about this river?

   _____

3. How does it rank in comparison to other rivers?

   _____

4. What is the Congo River's other name?

   _____

5. What is Equatorial Guinea's chief export crop?

   _____

6. What is the capital city of Congo?

   _____

The Rain Forest (cont.)

Find information about this area in reference books and answer these questions.

7. Name four animals that live in the African rain forest.

   1. _____   3. _____

   2. _____   4. _____

8. From what European country did the people of Equatorial Guinea win their freedom?

   _____
   _____
   _____
   _____

9. What primitive ethnic group is associated with the African rain forest?

   _____
   _____
   _____
   _____

10. Why is the African rain forest in less trouble than the South American rain forests?

   _____
   _____
   _____
   _____

African Fact Game

This game can be played in different ways:

Game 1—You can use a Jeopardy format. Students love this, and they can set it up all by themselves or with just a little help. Run the answer cards on one color of paper and the question cards on another color for easy sorting.

Game 2—You can make a card game like rummy. All the cards should be run on one color for this. Shuffle the cards and deal five to each player. Put the leftovers facedown or in the middle of the table. Players draw from the stack and discard in another stack. The object of the game is to lay down pairs by matching questions and answers. You can make it more complicated by allowing students to challenge one another's matched pairs if they think the matches are incorrect. Have students keep track of the rules they make and write game directions.

Fact Game Cards

It is the highest point in Africa	What is Mt. Kilimanjaro?
It has the largest area of any country in Africa.	What is Sudan?
It has the most people of any country in Africa.	What is Nigeria?

African Fact Game (cont.)

Fact Game Cards (cont.)

It is the second largest continent.	What is Africa?
It is the longest river on Earth	What is the Nile?
It is one of the wettest places on Earth.	What is the Congo Basin?
It is the name of the cape at the southern tip of Africa?	What is the Cape of Good Hope?
These animals are hunted for their tusks and horns.	What are elephants and rhinoceroses?
It is a large island off the southeast coast of Africa.	What is Madagascar?

African Fact Game (cont.)

Fact Game Cards (cont.)

It is the largest desert in the world.	What is the Sahara?
It is a place in the desert where water and plants are found.	What is an oasis?
It is the bean from which chocolate is made.	What is cacao?
They are people who move from place to place to find water and grazing land.	What are nomads?
It is the capital city of Egypt.	What is Cairo?
They are a pride.	What is a group of lions called?

African Fact Game (cont.)

Fact Game Cards (cont.)

They are animals that are used for transportation in the desert.	What are camels?
It is an area of heavy rain forest.	What is the Congo Basin?
They are people who hunt endangered animals illegally	What are poachers?
Lake Assal, Djibouti, at 512 feet (155 m) below sea level.	What is the lowest point in Africa?
The place where archaeologists have found important fossils.	What is Olduvai Gorge?
It is the primary language of North Africa.	What is Arabic?

African Fact Game (cont.)

Fact Game Cards (cont.)

Let your students make their own question-and-answer fact cards. Students usually like to make extra hard ones in hopes of stumping each other, so have them write the book and page number where the information can be found for each card.

	Book:_____ Page:_____
	Book:_____ Page:_____
	Book:_____ Page:_____
	Book:_____ Page:_____
	Book:_____ Page:_____

The Geography Center

Putting the Center Together

You can set up your Geography Center in a corner of your classroom and make it as simple or as elaborate as you want. The center should have a map, a globe, and an atlas. (Several maps, a couple of globes, and multiple copies of the atlas would be even better.) A table and chairs will facilitate group activities and discussions. A supply of writing and drawing materials will also come in handy. A bookcase, shelf, or window sill can be utilized for storing reference books. The more reference books you can provide, the better the assigned projects will be. If you have access to a TV, VCR, and tapes, you can show movies about the places you are studying. There are many tapes of this variety available, and the visual learners in your class will really appreciate this. Cushions for sitting on the floor to read or view tapes add a cozy touch.

Making the Center Work

You can make the Geography Center part of your instructional day by scheduling groups to do center work. Change the materials daily or weekly or provide a set of task cards at the beginning of the unit and expect each student to work through them individually or as part of a group. (See pages 53–55.)

Use Portfolios

Have students make portfolios and store them in containers in an accessible area of your center. Try using the inexpensive but sturdy plastic crates that are available at local hardware stores. Make students responsible for their own progress by having them file their own work, both completed work and work in progress. Have students create attractive covers for their portfolios so the accumulated work can be attractively displayed at your school's open house.

Deck the Walls

Encourage artwork, creative writing, and exploratory math to go along with your geography unit and spread it throughout the curriculum. Display these products on a bulletin board in your Geography Center. Have students mount and post their own work. They can cut out letters and create colorful captions for the board.

Have another bulletin board reserved for posting newspaper and magazine articles dealing with the continent you are studying. Encourage your students to bring in these articles, share them, and discuss their meaning and importance.

The Geography Center (cont.)

Task Cards

Task Card #3
What is the highest mountain peak on the continent?

How tall is it?

In which country is it found?

Task Card #4
What is the largest country on the continent?

What countries or bodies of water border it?

What is its capital city?

Task Card #1
What is the longest river on the continent?

How long is it?

Through which country or countries does it flow?

Task Card #2
What is the most important mountain range on the continent?

How long is it?

In which country or countries are these mountains found?

©1995 Teacher Created Materials, Inc. 53 #695 Africa

The Geography Center (cont.)

Task Cards (cont.)

Task Card #5

What is the smallest country on the continent?

What countries or bodies of water border it?

What is its capital city?

Task Card #6

What is the largest lake on the continent?

In which country or countries is it found?

Which river is associated with it?

Task Card #7

What animals are associated with the continent?

In what country or countries do they live?

Are they in any danger in today's civilization?

Task Card #8

What variations in climate are found on the continent?

What variations in weather are found on the continent?

Can people live in all parts of the continent?

The Geography Center (cont.)

Task Card Response

Leave a stack of these task card response forms in the geography center for students to use.

Name _____ Date _____

Task Card # _____

Question #1

_____
_____
_____
_____

Question #2

_____
_____
_____
_____

Question #3

_____
_____
_____

Bonus

I also learned _____
_____
_____
_____

The Culminating Activity: Making a Book

Method

You and your students can go about bookmaking in many different ways. Here are some suggestions:

- The book can be your students' showcase portfolios.
- Students can review and reflect upon the work they have accumulated in their portfolios, select the most representative samples or the pieces they like best, and put these things together in book form.
- The book can be a showcase portfolio based on the teacher's criteria.
- Have students select work from their portfolios based on a list you develop.
- The book can be comprised of new material that sums up the unit.
- Have students complete various assignments meant specifically for inclusion in their books, showing their grasp of the material. (See pages 57–67.)

Contents

In most cases you will probably want your students to include maps, facts about both physical and political geography, research about animals, people, and resources. They can review or report on any books they have read about the continent, and they can write about what they have learned and how it has affected the way they view the world.

Cover

You can specify and provide the design for the cover so that all of the books will be uniform, or you can encourage your students to design a cover that is representative of the continent. A collage of pictures cut from magazines and travel brochures is an option that works well.

Be sure to laminate the finished covers so the books can be used as part of your classroom library or Geography Center reference shelf. Your students may also want to share their books with students in other classes.

Exciting ideas for binding and publishing follow on pages 68–70.

The Culminating Activity: Making a Book (cont.)

Trace an outline map of the continent. Transfer information about its physical features from all of the maps you have made. You might want to use different colors to create a key.

Name _____ Date _____

Map of Physical Features

The Culminating Activity: Making a Book *(cont.)*

Use the information you have already gathered or do some new research to complete this page.

Name _____ Date _____

Facts About Physical Features

Area: _____

_____

Highest Point: _____

_____

Lowest Point: _____

_____

Largest Island: _____

_____

Longest River: _____

_____

Largest Lake: _____

_____

Tallest Waterfall: _____

_____

Largest Desert: _____

_____

Longest Reef: _____

_____

The Culminating Activity: Making a Book (cont.)

Trace an outline map of the continent. Transfer information about its political features from all of the maps you have made. You might want to use a numbered list to create a key.

Name _____ Date _____

Map of Political Features

The Culminating Activity: Making a Book (cont.)

Use the information you have already gathered or do some new research to complete this page.

Name _____ Date _____

Facts About Political Features

Population: _____

Largest Country (by area): _____

Largest Country (by population): _____

Smallest Country (by area): _____

Smallest Country (by population): _____

Largest Metropolitan Area (by population): _____

_____

_____

_____

_____

_____

Newest Countries: _____

_____

_____

_____

_____

_____

#695 Africa   ©1995 Teacher Created Materials, Inc.

The Culminating Activity: Making a Book (cont.)

Use the information you have already gathered or do some new research to complete this page.

Name _____ Date_____

The People

The people of this continent belong to these ethnic groups:

_____

_____

_____

They speak these languages:

_____

_____

_____

They live in these different environments:

_____

_____

_____

Their ways of life have changed or are changing:

_____

_____

_____

_____

The Culminating Activity: Making a Book (cont.)

Pick the city on the continent that is most interesting to you. Use the information you have already gathered or do some new research to complete this page.

Name _____ Date _____

The city of _____.

This city is in _____

Area: _____

Population: _____
_____

Language(s): _____
_____

Ethnic Groups: _____
_____

Religious Groups: _____
_____

Famous Natural Features: _____
_____
_____

Famous Constructed Features: _____
_____
_____
_____
_____

The Culminating Activity: Making a Book (cont.)

Use the information you have already gathered or do some new research to complete this page.

Name _____ Date _____

The Animals

The best known animals of this continent are _____
_____
_____

The animals of this continent are important because _____
_____
_____

The animals that still live in their natural habitats are _____
_____
_____

The animals that are on the endangered list are _____
_____
_____

They are on the endangered list because _____
_____
_____
_____

©1995 Teacher Created Materials, Inc.   #695 Africa

The Culminating Activity: Making a Book (cont.)

Keep track of the books you read about the continent on this log.

Name _____ Date _____

Book Log

Title: _____	Fiction: _____
Author: _____	Nonfiction: _____
Illustrator: _____	Rating: _____

Title: _____	Fiction: _____
Author: _____	Nonfiction: _____
Illustrator: _____	Rating: _____

Title: _____	Fiction: _____
Author: _____	Nonfiction: _____
Illustrator: _____	Rating: _____

Title: _____	Fiction: _____
Author: _____	Nonfiction: _____
Illustrator: _____	Rating: _____

The Culminating Activity: Making a Book *(cont.)*

Use copies of this form to review your favorite nonfiction books about the continent you have been studying.

Name _____ Date _____

Book Review/Nonfiction

Title: _____

Author: _____

Illustrator: _____

Summary: _____

_____

_____

_____

_____

_____

Reasons I liked or did not like this book: _____

_____

_____

_____

_____

_____

_____

Bonus!

If you liked this book and think other people should read it, you can do one of two things. (1) Write a paragraph or two telling how a nonfiction book can help you understand a continent or a country and post it on the bulletin board in the Geography Center. (2) Make a poster advertising the book and post it on the bulletin board in the Geography Center.

The Culminating Activity: Making a Book (cont.)

Use copies of this form to review your favorite fiction books about the continent you have been studying.

Name _____ Date _____

Book Review/Fiction

Title: _____

Author: _____

Illustrator: _____

Summary: _____

_____

_____

_____

_____

_____

Reasons I liked or did not like this book: _____

_____

_____

_____

_____

_____

Bonus!

If you liked this book and think other people should read it, you can do one of two things. (1) Write a paragraph or two telling how a fiction book can help you understand a continent or a country and post it on the bulletin board in the Geography Center. (2) Make a poster advertising the book and post it on the bulletin board in the Geography Center.

The Culminating Activity: Making a Book *(cont.)*

Write a reflective essay in which you discuss the ways that studying geography has given you a better understanding of the world and the people in it.

Name _____ Date _____

Title: _____

The Culminating Activity: Making a Book *(cont.)*

Book Binding Ideas

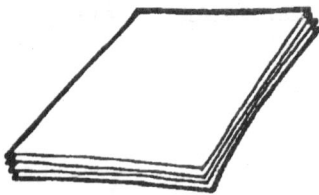

1. Stack all the pages of the book in a neat pile.

3. Leaving approximately 1/2" (1.25 cm) border, staple or sew all of the pages together on the left side.

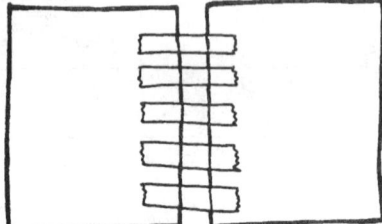

5. Leaving approximately 1" (2.5 cm) between them, tape the cardboard pieces together.

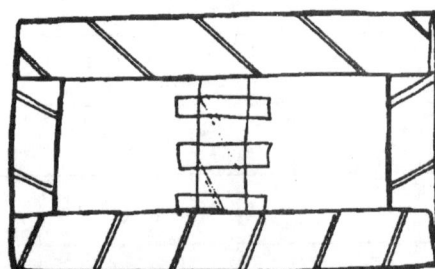

7. Fold up the edges of material over the cardboard and glue in place.

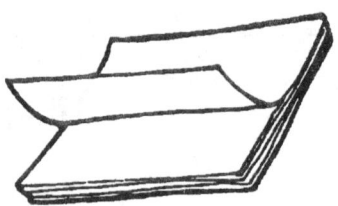

2. Place a blank sheet of paper on the top and bottom of the pages.

4. Place two pieces of lightweight cardboard side by side. (Cereal boxes work well.) Each piece should be 1/2 to 1" (1.25 to 2.5 cm) larger than the size of the pages in the book.

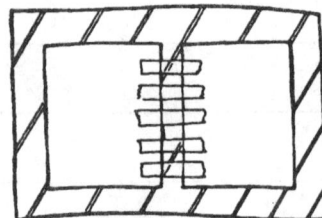

6. Put the cardboard on top of your covering material (e.g., fabric, wallpaper, contact paper, or wrapping paper). Glue the cardboard and covering material together, leaving a 1 to 1 1/2" (2.5 to 3.25 cm) material border.

8. Glue the blank pages to the inside of the cardboard covers. Your book is ready to read and share.

The Culminating Activity: Making a Book (cont.)

Pop-Up Books

1. Fold a 8 1/2" x 11" (22 cm x 28 cm) piece of paper in half crosswise.

2. Measure and mark 2 3/4" (7 cm) from each side along the fold. Cut 2 3/4" (7 cm) slits at the marks.

3. Push cut area inside-out and crease to form the pop-up section.

4. Draw, color, and cut out the object to get "popped-up."

5. Glue it onto the pop-up section.

6. Glue two pages back to back, making sure the pop-up section is free.

7. Glue additional pages together, making as many pages (including pop-up pages) as you like. Be sure to include a free sheet on both the front and back so that those pages can be glued to a cover.

8. Glue a cover over the entire book.

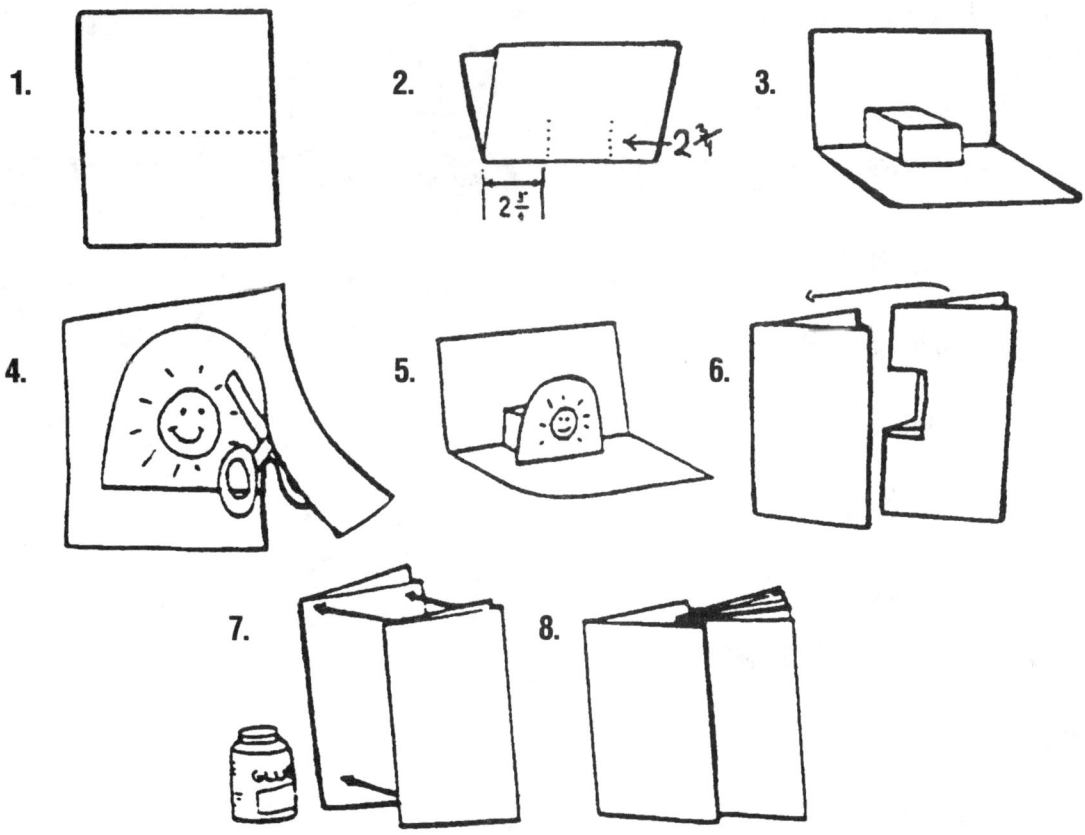

The Culminating Activity: Making a Book (cont.)

Real Markets for Student Writing

Student writing can be sent to the following addresses. Check your professional journals for more sources.

Children's Playmate (ages 5–8)
P.O. Box 567B
Indianapolis, Indiana 46206

Cricket (ages 6–12)
Cricket League
P.O. Box 300
Peru, Illinois 61354

Ebony Jr! (ages 6–12)
820 S. Michigan Avenue
Chicago, Illinois 60605

Flying Pencil Press (ages 8–14)
P.O. Box 7667
Elgin, Illinois 60121

Highlights for Children (ages 2–11)
803 Church Street
Honesdale, Pennsylvania 18431

Jack and Jill (ages 8–12)
P.O. Box 567B
Indianapolis, Indiana 46206

Stone Soup (ages 5–14)
P.O. Box 83
Santa Cruz, California 95063

National Written and Illustrated by...
(This is an awards contest for students in all grade levels. Write for rules and guidelines.)
Landmark Editions, Inc.
P.O. Box 4469
Kansas City, Missouri 64127

Glossary

absolute location—See exact location.

altiplano—a high plateau or valley between higher mountains; particularly the high plain where the Andes divide in Peru and Bolivia

altitude—the height of land above the level of the sea

Antarctic Circle—an imaginary circle parallel to the equator and 23 degrees 30' from the South Pole.

aquifer—an underground reservoir of water contained within a porous rock layer

archipelago—a group or chain of islands

Arctic Circle—an imaginary circle parallel to the equator and 23 degrees 30' from the North Pole.

atoll—a ring of coral islands encircling a lagoon

axis—an imaginary line that runs through the center of the Earth from the North Pole to the South Pole

basin—an area of land that is surrounded by higher land

bay—a body of water having land on at least two sides

boundary—a line on a map that separates one country from another

canal—a waterway dug across land for ships to go through

canyon—a deep valley with steep sides

cape—a piece of land that extends into a river, lake, or ocean

cardinal directions—the four main points of the compass: north, south, east, and west

cargo—a load of products carried from one place to another

cartographer—a map maker

channel—a waterway between two land masses; also, the part of a river that is deepest and carries the most water

climate—the kind of weather a region has over a long period of time

communication—the sending out of ideas and information; the means by which people do this

compass rose—the drawing that shows the directions of north, south, east, and west on a map

conservation—preserving valuable resources

continent—one of the seven main land masses on the earth's surface: North America, South America, Europe, Asia, Africa, Australia, and Antarctica

continental divide—the geographic area that separates the direction in which water currents flow

continental shelf—the shallow, gently sloping sea floor that surrounds each continent

Glossary (cont.)

country—the territory of a nation, marked by a boundary that separates it from other nations

current—a fast-moving stream of water in the ocean

degree—one 360th part of the circumference of a circle; used as a unit of measurement

delta—an area of silt, sand, and gravel deposited at the mouth of a river

deposit—a large area of mineral deep in the Earth

desert—a very dry area of land covered with rocks and/or sand

distance scale—a measuring line on a map that helps to figure out the distance from one place to another

dormant volcano—a temporarily inactive volcano

drought—a long period without rain

economic activity—a way that people use their resources to live

ecosystem—a system formed by the interaction of living organisms with each other and with their environment

environment—the surroundings in which everything lives

equator—the imaginary line that circles the middle of the earth, halfway between the North Pole and the South Pole

erosion—the wearing away of land by the elements (ice, sun, water, and wind)

escarpment—a cliff separating two nearly flat land surfaces that lie at different levels

estuary—the widening mouth of a river where it meets the sea; tides ebb and flow within this area

exact location—the location of a point which can be given in latitude and longitude, also called absolute location

extinct volcano—a totally inactive volcano

fertile—good for growing plants and crops

fjord—a narrow, steep-sided ocean inlet that reaches far into a coastline

forest—a large area covered with trees and undergrowth

frontier—land that is mostly unsettled

geothermal power—energy from heat within the Earth

geyser—a hot spring that shoots water and steam into the air

Glossary (cont.)

glacier—a large, thick, slow moving mass of ice

globe—a round model of the Earth

gorge—a deep, narrow passage between mountains

grassland—a wide area covered with grass and an occasional tree

grid—a series of evenly spaced lines used to locate places on a map

grove—a large field of trees

growing season—the period of time in which the weather is warm enough for crops to grow

gulf—an area of sea that is partly surrounded by land

harbor—a body of water sheltered by natural or artificial barriers and deep enough to moor ships

hemisphere—half of a sphere; on a globe, a hemisphere represents one half of the Earth

highland—an area of hills or mountains

humid—moist or damp

hurricane—a fierce storm of wind and rain

hydroelectric power—electric energy produced by water power

iceberg—a huge chunk of ice floating in the sea

ice sheet—a broad, thick layer of glacial ice that covers a wide area

irrigation—supplying water to dry land through pipes, ditches, or canals

island—a piece of land entirely surrounded by water

isthmus—a narrow strip of land that connects two larger landmasses and has water on both sides

jungle—a hot, humid area of land which is overgrown with trees and other plants

key—the section that explains the symbols used on a map

lagoon—a shallow body of water that opens on the sea but is protected by a sandbar or coral reef

lake—a body of water completely surrounded by land

landform—a shape of land, such as a mountain, valley, or plateau

Glossary (cont.)

landforms map—a map that uses colors to show the height and shape of the land; also called a contour map

landlocked country—a country surrounded by land without access to the sea

landmark—an important thing or place that stands out from everything around it

latitude line—an east-west line drawn parallel to the equator on a globe

lava—hot, liquid rock

location—the position of a point on the surface of the earth; can be exact or relative

longitude line—a north-south line drawn from pole to pole on a globe

lowland—a low, flat area of land

manufacturing—making finished goods from raw materials

map—a drawing of all or part of the earth's surface showing where things are located

meridian—any of the lines of longitude running north and south on a globe or map and representing a great circle of the Earth that passes through the poles

mesa—a broad, flat-topped landform with steep sides found in arid or semiarid regions

mineral—a natural occurring substance found on the earth

mining—the process of taking mineral deposits from the earth

moisture—water or other liquids in the air or on the ground; wetness

monsoon—a wind that produces wet and dry seasons in southern and eastern Asia

moor—an open expanse of rolling land covered with grass or other low vegetation

moraine—an accumulation of debris carried and deposited by a glacier

mountain—a large mass of land that rises high above the surrounding land

mountain range—a group or series of mountains

mouth—the place where a river empties into a larger body of water

natural gas—a light mineral often used for fuel; usually found near petroleum

natural resource—something occurring in nature that people need or want

North Pole—the point located at the most northern place on a globe

oasis—a place in the desert where water from underground springs allows plants to grow

ocean—a large body of salt water that covers much of the earth's surface

ore—a mixture of rock, soil, and minerals

outback—the remote backcountry of Australia

Glossary *(cont.)*

parallel—any of the imaginary lines parallel to the equator and representing degrees of latitude on the Earth's surface

peninsula—a body of land almost completely surrounded by water

petroleum—an oily liquid mineral

place—an area having characteristics that define them and make them different from other areas

plain—a low, flat land area

plateau—an area of flat land higher than the land around it

pollution—damage to air, water, or land by smoke, dust, or chemicals

population—all of the people who live in a particular place

population density—the number of people living in each square mile or kilometer of an area

port—a place where ships can load

prairie—a large area of flat land covered with tall, thick grass

preservation—keeping things safe from damage or destruction

prime meridian (Greenwich Meridian)—the special longitude line that is the starting point for measuring all the other lines of longitude

projection—a way of transferring the features of the Earth as represented on a globe to a flat piece of paper (map); the resulting style of map

rain forest—dense forest mostly composed of broadleaved evergreens found in wet tropical regions

ravine—a narrow valley with steep sides

raw material—a material in its natural state, used for making finished goods

reef—a narrow ridge of rock, sand, or coral just above or below the surface of the water

region—an area having distinctive characteristics that make it different from the surrounding areas

relative location—the location of a point on the earth's surface in relation to other points

reservoir—a lake or pond where water is stored for future use

resource—a supply of valuable or useful things such as water, coal, soil, forests, or air; see natural resource

revolution—the movement of the Earth in orbit around the sun; one complete revolution equals a year

river—a large stream of water flowing in a channel

rotation—the movement of the earth turning on its axis; one complete rotation equals 24 hours

rural—away from cities and close to farms

Glossary (cont.)

savanna—a tropical grassland with scattered trees

scale—the ratio of map distance to actual distance on the Earth's surface

sea—a large body of salt water

sound—a long, broad ocean inlet usually parallel to the coast, or a long stretch of water separating an island from the mainland

South Pole—the point located at the most southern place on a globe

state—the strongest governing body, subordinate to a national government (Not to be confused with the nation-state.)

steppe—a grassland in the temperate zone where limited rainfall prevents tree growth

strait—a narrow waterway that connects two seas

swamp—a lowland area covered with shallow water and dense vegetation

symbol—something that stands for a real thing

temperature—the measure of how hot or cold a place is

territory—a region that is owned or controlled by another country or political unit

time zone—one of 24 areas or zones of the Earth in which the time is one hour earlier than in the zone to its east

tributary—a river or stream that flows into a larger body of water

transportation—the way in which people or goods travel or are moved from one place to another

Tropic of Cancer—the parallel of latitude that lies 23 degrees 27' north of the equator

Tropic of Capricorn—the parallel of latitude that lies 23 degrees 27' south of the equator

tundra—a wide, treeless arctic plain where few plants or animals live because of frozen subsoil called permafrost

---

urban sea—the city and its surrounding built-up area

valley—a long, low area between hills or mountains

volcano—an opening in the earth's surface through which hot liquid rock (magma) and other materials are forced out

---

weather—the condition of the air at a certain time or place

Software Review

Software: *Where in the World Is Carmen Sandiego?* (Broderbund)

Hardware: 640K IBM PC with color graphics card, color monitor, sound card, and CD-ROM drive or 4MB Macintosh with CD-ROM drive

Grade Level: Intermediate

Summary: *Where in the World Is Carmen Sandiego?* is a simulation program where students will learn about world geography and world history. Carmen Sandiego and her group of villains are stealing priceless artifacts from around the world. It is the job of your students to recover the stolen artifacts, return them to their country of origin, and arrest the criminals responsible. By following clues and interviewing witnesses, your students will be able to track down the criminals.

Included in this software package is The World Almanac and Book of Facts to help students interpret clues and locate various places around the world. Students will be promoted as they solve cases, and when they have solved eighty cases, they will be retired from active duty.

Bibliography

Aardema, Verna. *Anansi Finds a Fool: An Ashanti Tale*. Dial, 1992.

Aardema, Verna. *Sebgugugu the Glutton: A Bantu Tale from Rwanda, Africa.* Eerdmans, 1993.

African Tales: Folklore of the Central African Republic. Telecraft, 1992.

Anderson, David. *The Origin of Life on Earth: An African Creation Myth.* Sights, 1991.

Arkhurst, Joyce Cooper. *The Adventures of Spider: West African Folktales*. Little, 1992.

Berger, Terry. *Black Fairy Tales.* Macmillan, 1974.

Brill, Marlene. *Libya.* Childrens, 1988.

Chaisson, John. *African Journey.* Macmillan, 1987.

Crossland, Bert. "Where on Earth Are We?" Book Links. September, 1994

Dickinson, Mary B. (Ed.). *National Geographic Picture Atlas of Our World*. National Geographic Society, 1993

Fox, Mary V. *Tunisia.* Childrens, 1990.

Geographic Education National Implementation Project. Guidelines, 1987.

Georges, D.V. *Africa.* Childrens, 1986.

Ghana in Pictures. Lerner, 1988.

Greeves, Nick. *When Hippo Was Hairy: And Other Tales from Africa.* Barron's, 1988.

Halliburton, Warren J. *Africa's Struggle to Survive.* Macmillan, 1993.

Halliburton, Warren J. *African Landscapes*. Macmillan, 1993.

Halliburton, Warren J. *City and Village Life.* Macmillan, 1993.

Hintz, Martin. *Morocco.* Childrens, 1985.

Jacobsoen, Karen. *Kenya*. Childrens, 1991.

Kurtz, Jane. *Ethiopia: The Roof of Africa.* Macmillan, 1991.

Laure, Jason. *Angola.* Childrens, 1993.

Laure, Jason. *Namibia.* Childrens, 1993.

Laure, Jason. *Zambia.* Childrens, 1989.

Levy, Patricia. *Nigeria.* Marshall Cavendish, 1993.

McCulla, Patricia. *Tanzania.* Chelsea, 1988.

McKissack, Patricia. *Monkey-Monkey's Trick: Based on an African Folk Tale.* Random, 1988.

Paton, Jonathan. *The Land and People of South Africa.* Harper, 1988.

Percefull, Aaron W. *The Nile.* Watts, 1984.

South Africa in Pictures. Lerner, 1988.

Stanley, Diane and Peter Vennema. *Shaka: King of the Zulus.* Morrow, 1988.

Stewart, Gail B. *Liberia.* Macmillan, 1992.

Timberlake, Lloyd. *Feminine in Africa.* Watts, 1986.

Walter, Mildred P. *Brother to the Wind.* Lothrop, 1985.

Bibliography *(cont.)*

Technology

Broderbund. *MacGlobe & PC Globe.* Available from Learning Services, (800)877-9378. disk

Broderbund. *Where in the World Is Carmen Sandiego?* Available from Troll (800)526-5289. CD-ROM and disk

Bureau of Electronic Publishing Inc. *World Fact Book.* Available from Educational Resources, (800)624-2926. CD-ROM

CLEARVUE. *The Earth, the Oceans, and Plants & Animals: Interactive, curriculum oriented CD-ROMs.* Available from Educational Resources, (800)624-2926. CD-ROM

DeLorme Publishing. *Global Explorer.* Available from DeLorme Publishing, 1995. CD-ROM

Impressions. *My First World Atlas.* Available from Educational Resources, (800)624-2926. disk

Lawrence. *Nigel's World Adventures in World Geography.* Available from Educational Resources, (800)624-2926. CD-ROM and disk

Magic Quest. *Time Treks and Earth Treks.* Available from Educational Resources, (800)624-2926. disk

MECC. *World GeoGraph.* Available from Educational Resources, (800)624-2926. disk

Mindscape. *World Atlas.* Available from Educational Resources, (800)624-2926. disk

National Geographic. *STV: World Geography.* Available from National Geographic Educational Technology, (800)328-2936. videodisc

National Geographic. *Zip Zap Map.* Available from Educational Resources, (800)624-2926. laserdisc and disk

Newton Technology. *GEOvista Tutor.* Available from William K. Bradford, (800)421-2009. disk

Orange Cherry. *Jungle Safari.* Available from Educational Resources, (800) 624-2926. disk

Orange Cherry. *Time Traveler.* Available from Educational Resources, (800)624-2926. CD-ROM

Pride in Learning. *Global Issues.* Available from Educational Resources, (800)624-2926. disk

Queue. *Atlas Explorer.* Available from Educational Resources, (800)624-2926. disk

Sanctuary Woods. *Ecology Treks.* Available from Learning Services, (800)624-2926. software and videodisc

Software Toolworks. *World Atlas.* Available from Learning Services, (800)877-9378. CD-ROM and disk

SVE. *Geography on Laserdisc.* Available from Learning Services, (800)877-9378. laserdisc.

Soleil. *Zurk's Learning Safari.* Available from Educational Resources, (800)624-2926. disk

Answer Key

Page 161

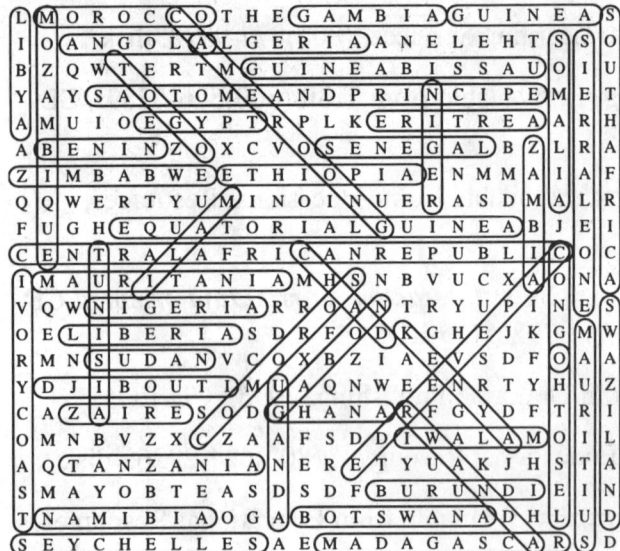

Page 174

1. gorillas
2. giraffe
3. camel
4. elephant
5. lion
6. leopard
7. aardvark
8. hippopotamus
9. rhinoceros
10. baboon
11. zebra
12. antelope
13. ringtailed lemur
14. crocodile
15. chimpanzee

Pages 191–192

1. 2,900 miles (4,640 km)
2. no delta
3. 4th longest, 2nd in volume of water carried
4. the Zaire River
5. cacao
6. Brazzaville
7. (answers will vary)
8. Spain
9. the Pygmies
10. (answers will vary)